snapshot·picture·library

KITTENS

snapshot·picture·library

KITTENS

FOG CITY PRESS

Published by Fog City Press,
a division of Weldon Owen Inc.
415 Jackson Street
San Francisco, CA 94111
www.weldonowen.com

WELDON OWEN GROUP
Chief Executive Officer John Owen
Chief Financial Officer Simon Fraser

WELDON OWEN INC.
President, Chief Executive Officer Terry Newell
Vice President, International Sales Stuart Laurence
Vice President, Sales and New Business Development Amy Kaneko
Vice President, Sales—Asia and Latin America Dawn Low
Vice President, Publisher Roger Shaw
Vice President, Creative Director Gaye Allen
Managing Editor, Fog City Press Karen Perez
Assistant Editor Sonia Vallabh
Art Director Kelly Booth
Designer Andreas Schueller
Design Assistant Justin Hallman
Production Director Chris Hemesath
Production Manager Michelle Duggan
Sales Manager Emily Bartle
Color Manager Teri Bell

Text Karen Penzes
Picture Research Brandi Valenza

A WELDON OWEN PRODUCTION
© 2007 Weldon Owen Inc.

Library of Congress Control Number: 2007937435

ISBN-13: 978-1-74089-638-2
ISBN-10: 1-74089-638-6

10 9 8 7 6 5 4 3 2

Color separations by Sang Choy International, Singapore.
Printed by Tien Wah Press in Singapore.

Have you ever had a kitten
curl up in your lap for a nap?
Or felt the tongue of a kitten
when it licked you? Kittens
are warm little balls of joy that
love to snuggle, romp, and play
wherever they are.

From playing hide-and-seek
to climbing up on the roof or
curling up under your blankets,
these kittens are up to all sorts
of mischievous adventures!

When they are very young, kittens like to stay with their brothers and sisters.

As they get older, kittens set out to explore and hunt...

...and maybe
even catch some
fluffy clouds!

Kittens come in
many colors—
gray, orange,
white, brown—
sometimes all
mixed together.

Even kittens
in the same
family can
have different
markings from
each other.

Kittens love to play peekaboo
and find odd spots to hide.

But if they meow,
they might
give away their
hiding spots!

So much
exploring
and playing
can tire a
kitten out.

But it's not long
before they find
another adventure!

Just like us,
kittens use their
noses to sniff
all the smells
around them.

And their
wide eyes
are great
for examining
the world.

What can this
little kitten see?

Kittens can find all sorts of spots to hide— under a rug, a hole in the ground, or even under a paw!

Having places
to hide makes
kittens feel safe.

Sometimes you can catch curious kittens climbing walls, rolling around, or even getting a little cheeky—watch out for that pink tongue!

Kittens are all born with blue eyes. Their eyes change color as they get older.

You can find kittens with long hair, short hair, and medium hair.

And you can find kittens in
boxes and wide-brimmed hats!

Or even inside
a big bucket!

Everywhere little kittens go there are new places to explore— up high, down low...

...on top,
and everywhere
in between.

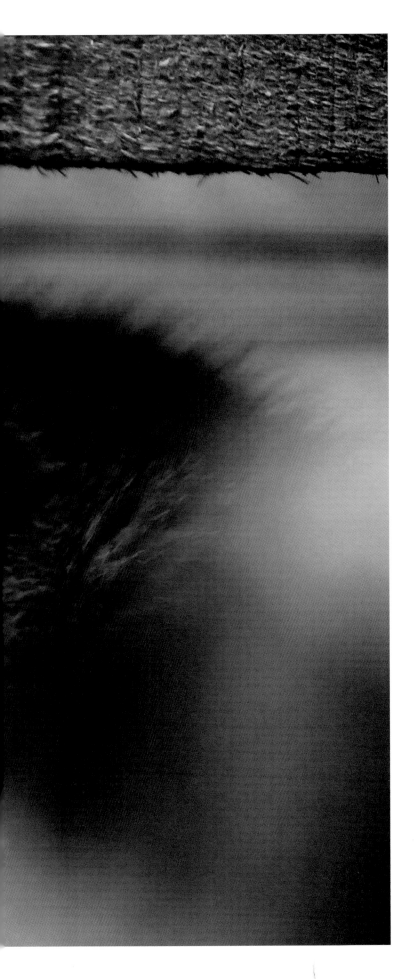

Such a big world can be scary for a kitten...

...but they
soon learn to
climb trees—
or even a rat's
cage!

A group of
kittens born
from the same
mother at the
same time is
called a litter.

Kittens from the
same litter often
learn about the
world together.

For example,
they might
learn that
pianos can
make a lot
of noise!

And after a long day of discoveries and frisky romps, there's nothing better than finding a good place to nap.

Would you like to
snuggle with me?

ACKNOWLEDGMENTS

Weldon Owen would like to thank the following people for their assistance in the production of this book: Diana Heom, Ashley Martinez, Danielle Parker, Lucie Parker, Phil Paulick, and Erin Zaunbrecher.

CREDITS

Key t=top; b=bottom; DT=Dreamstime; iSP=iStockphoto; LO=Lucky Oliver; SST=Shutterstock

2 iSP; 5 DT; z SST; 9 SST; 10 SST; 11t iSP, b LO; 12 SST; 14t DT, b LO;15 DT; 17 SST; 18 DT; 19 SST; 21 SST; 22 DT; 23t DT, b LO; 25 DT; 26t DT, b LO; 27 DT; 28 iSP; 29t DT, b DT; 31 SST; 32t DT, b DT; 33 DT; 35 iSP; 36t DT, bDT; 37 DT; 38 SST; 40 LO; 41t iSP, biSP; 42 iSP; 43 iSP; 45 SST; 46t DT, biSP; 47 DT; 48 DT; 49t DT, b DT; 50 SST; 52 DT; 53t DT, b LO; 54t LO, b SST; 55 iSP; 57 SST; 58 DT; 59t DT, b DT; 60 iSP; 61t DT, b DT; 63 SST; 64 DT